Table of Contents

Amphibians with Gills

Mudpuppies are
slimy skinned amphibians.
They breathe underwater
with their bushy red gills.

gills

Mudpuppies are gray, red, or brown with dark spots. They grow 8 to 17 inches (20 to 43 centimeters) long.

Mudpuppies have
long, flat-sided tails.
Their tails swish as they swim.
Tiny toes on their feet
help them walk underwater.

Where Mudpuppies Live

Mudpuppies live in streams,

rivers, and lakes.

They are found

in the eastern United States

and southeastern Canada.

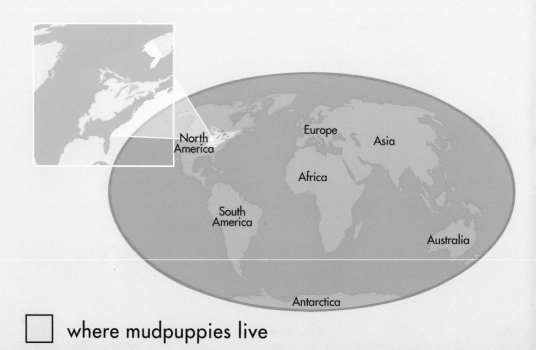

North America
Europe
Asia
Africa
South America
Australia
Antarctica

where mudpuppies live

Days and Nights

During the day, mudpuppies
hide under rocks and logs.
The hiding mudpuppies
stay safe from fish, snakes,
birds, and other predators.

At night, it is time

for mudpuppies to hunt.

They hunt crayfish, worms,

and underwater insects.

15

Hunting mudpuppies
walk slowly, sniffing for prey.
When the prey is close,
the mudpuppy sucks the prey
into its mouth.

A Mudpuppy's Life

A female mudpuppy lays

30 to 100 yellow eggs.

She stays close to her eggs

to protect them

from predators.

Mudpuppy Life Cycle

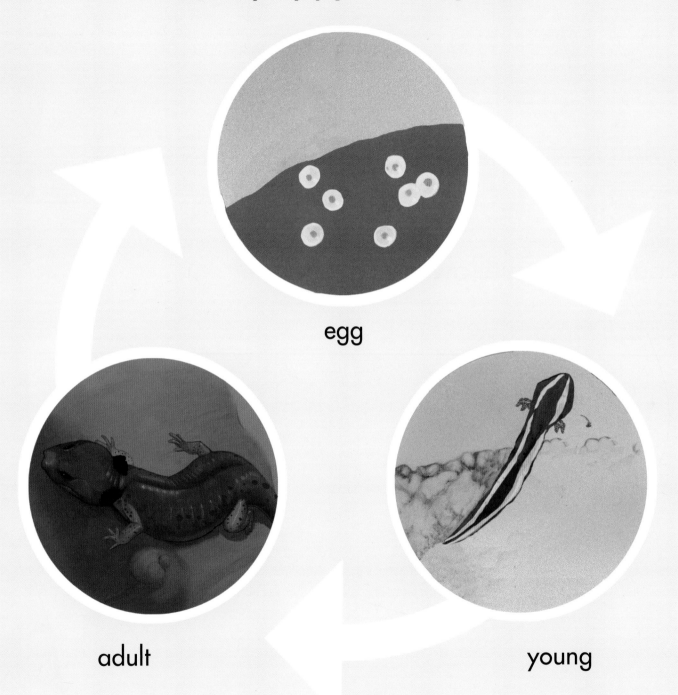

egg

young

adult

In a month or two,

the eggs hatch.

The young have yellow stripes.

Mudpuppies can live

for more than 30 years.

Glossary

crayfish — a small freshwater animal that looks like a lobster

gills — the organ on a fish's side used for breathing

hatch — to break open; mudpuppy eggs hatch in one to two months.

predator — an animal that hunts other animals for food

prey — an animal hunted by other animals for food

slimy — soft and slippery

swish — to move back and forth

Read More

Mattison, Christopher. *Reptiles and Amphibians.* Facts at Your Fingertips. Redding, Conn.: Brown Bear, 2006.

Theodorou, Rod. *Amphibians.* Animal Babies. Chicago: Heinemann, 2007.

Internet Sites

FactHound offers a safe, fun way to find Internet sites related to this book. All of the sites on FactHound have been researched by our staff.

Here's all you do:

Visit *www.facthound.com*

FactHound will fetch the best sites for you!

Index

Word Count: 170

Grade: 1

Early-Intervention Level: 17